CW00558321

HOW TO ACCESS YOUR DIVINE ENERGY

By

Chris Josh

CHRIS JOSH

www.ChrisJosh.com

Copyright ©2024 Chris Josh

All rights reserved

Get free, unique content periodically and be the first to know about new releases and exclusive offers.

Subscribe to the emails at **ChrisJosh.com/Subscribe**

Your email will never be shared or sold.

BOOKS BY CHRIS JOSH

CITY OF SERPENTS

THE WINNING HABIT

UNLEASH YOUR CONFIDENCE

8000 ULTIMATE AFFIRMATIONS

HOW CHAMPIONS TALK TO THEMSELVES

Dedication

I dedicate this book to every authentic person in the world, who are always seeking knowledge and divinity. And to those who contribute positively to society and spread love everywhere they go. And to those who choose to forgive the ones who have wronged them.

Thank you to everyone who seeks the truth, spreads the truth and defends the truth. Thank you to those who refuse to sell their souls for any amount of money. And thank you to those who stand up for justice and stand up for the oppressed around the world.

Table of Contents

Introduction

Welcome to your divine energy! Here, you will find the path to a life full of unending miracles. You'll learn about the vibration scale and where you fall on it and how to move up the scale, as well as how your vibration is creating the life you've been experiencing. You'll also learn which habits need to go and which habits you need to adopt in order to be able to access your divine energy.

The last part of the book contains the basic contract and "The 10 Day Transformation Workbook," which is meant to help you restructure your days so that you can manifest your most joyful and prosperous life, full of electrified energy.

Chapter 1

The Vibration Scale

In order to access your divine energy, you must transform yourself from a low vibration to a much higher one. This means you must travel from the lowest vibration, which is shame, all the way to enlightenment and authenticity, which are one of the highest vibrations one can be in. Gratitude is an even higher vibration, second only to God consciousness. In short, you must transform yourself into a state of permanent gratitude, which means you have to accept your life now and the way it has played out so far. And it also means you must forgive everyone.

These are the different vibrational states with their corresponding values. The higher the value, the higher the vibration. The objective of this book is to help you move from the bottom of the scale to the uppermost part of the vibration scale. You can think of the lowest vibration as hell on Earth and the highest vibration as heaven on Earth.

God Consciousness 1000

Gratitude – Freedom – Empowerment 900

Appreciation – 780

Enlightenment – 700

Peace – 600

Joy – 540

Love, Happiness, Enthusiasm – 500

Reason, Hope, Optimism – 400

Willingness – 310

Neutrality, Boredom – 250

Courage – 200

Pride, Blame, Worry – 175

Anger – 150

Desire, Jealousy – 125

Fear – 100

Grief – 75

Apathy, Depression – 50

Guilt, Insecurity – 30

Shame, Unworthiness, Despair – 20

Death – 0

Growing up, I was mostly in a lower vibration because I was a victim of child abuse by my mother, who has narcissistic personality disorder (NPD). Unfortunately for me, I was her scapegoat, and I was the black sheep of the family. As early as 4 years old, the abuse started, and I was physically beaten and verbally abused multiple times a day, every day, for nearly two decades. And the harsh criticism and verbal abuse lasted over 3 decades.

I exhibited the following low vibration states of mind: shame, guilt, apathy, grief, fear, and anger due to my circumstances. It took me over 40 years to get myself out of those states. I was attracting a chaotic life and was nowhere near my divine energy then. I was suicidal at the age of 9 years old until I was 42 years old. I had no will or desire to live.

After dealing with my physically abusive mother for nearly 20 years, I then unknowingly got married to a woman who also has narcissistic personality disorder (NPD) for 20 years. She was covert and she abused me mentally and emotionally without me knowing what she was purposely doing to me. I ended up walking away and divorcing her for the sake of my mental, emotional and physical health.

I say all of this to illustrate the adverse effects a low vibration can have on one's overall health and will to live. There's simply no way you'll access your divine energy feeling this way. The lower vibration states block you from accessing your divine energy.

When I was in my late 30's, I stumbled on Buddhism. I was born a Muslim. I found Buddhism to be a great philosophy and it really helped me tremendously. It gave me the necessary tools to pull myself out of the darkness I was in. I embraced Buddhism and I identified as a Buddhist. However, I still identified as a Muslim. But it was around this time I also embraced Jesus Christ as God and son of God. Ultimately, I became an omnist, which means I recognize all the different faiths and philosophies.

Besides being a victim of child abuse and later, emotional reactive abuse by the woman I was married to, I was also a victim of constant bullying for years by many kids and adults. This left me feeling ashamed, which is quite literally the worst vibration to be in. Because I was feeling ashamed, the universe kept me in shame by producing scenarios that would perpetuate the feeling of shame. The best way I can describe vibrations is that the lowest is hell and the highest is paradise. Luckily, you can move up the vibration scale, and in this book, I'll show you how so you can access your divine energy and divine self, which is your higher self, which is God.

My mother was very unforgiving with her ruthless behavior towards me. She even had a big problem with the way I was breathing and would randomly uppercut my chin to force me to close my mouth. I would hear my teeth bang against each other. See, I had enlarged adenoids, so I couldn't breathe through my nose. She didn't care that I couldn't breathe through my nose. She wanted me to keep my mouth shut anyways.

I always felt guilty because I thought I was doing something wrong to deserve this ill treatment. I was always crying myself to sleep and grieving. I was in constant fear – not just inside our apartment, but everywhere I went. I was even scared to fall asleep because I had this belief that I was going to drop a few hundred feet down a pit. I don't know if that's some sort of PTSD symptom.

Everyone could sense I was on edge and in fight or flight mode. The kids (and adults) could smell the fear on me and because of that, I was the target of bullying because I was an easy target. Unfortunately, people pick on people who look weak. And yes, fear is a weakness. It makes you look weak, and it makes you mentally and physically weak as well.

Because of the vibration I was in, I found myself having 3-4 fights a day in grammar school. I'd then walk home and get beaten, scolded, and berated by my mother. I didn't know this back then, but whatever you're feeling, that's what the universe will match you up with. In other words, what you feel is what you attract. If you feel fear, the universe will give you a type of life that would keep you in a state of fear. And because I was in fear, life kept presenting me with scenarios and circumstances that perpetuated that fear.

I was unknowingly stuck in a vicious, chaotic cycle of violence and pain. Everything just seemed to always go wrong for me. Bad luck followed me everywhere. It's as if a black cloud was always hovering over me. I felt hated by life and everyone. I felt like it was me versus everyone. I had undiagnosed autism and ADHD which made matters worse.

If you've ever dealt with any form of abuse, betrayal, or trauma, you could be depressed and/or anxious. Depression is underlying anger and anxiety is essentially fear. Anger and fear, as previously mentioned, are both low vibrations to be in. So, in order to access your divine energy, you must heal from depression and anger. I discuss in great detail on how to heal depression, anxiety, trauma, abuse, and betrayals in my other book, "City of Serpents."

As previously mentioned, the lower vibrations are hell and the higher ones are heaven on Earth, or some call it paradise. It's important to let go of the things that cause you fear. For example, the mainstream media instills a lot of fear in people. It also triggers anger in people. Family and friends can cause you fear, worry, doubt, and stress. And they, too, can do things to cause you to be angry. It's very important to cut off all toxicity – whether it's people, places, and/or things.

One must be aware of their addiction to fear and anger. Many times, unknowingly, people check the news because deep down they're oddly addicted to the emotions they experience as a result of consuming news stories.

Knowing that depression is underlying anger, you must be aware that odds are, you're angry about how a situation panned out or how things are currently going in your life or how a person betrayed you. Ask yourself, is the anger productive in anyway? Is it improving the situation? Chances are, it's not. So, it's pointless to suppress your anger. If you're angry at someone, just know they're living their life and your depression isn't affecting them one bit.

Regarding your worries. Most of the times they're baseless because no one knows what's going to happen. You're constantly creating "what-if" scenarios. While you may be going about it logically, the reality is most of the scenarios you draw up simply don't materialize in the real world. Think back at all those times you worried something would happen and it never happened. It's pointless to worry. You must shift your focus on the present moment. It's called the present for a reason – it's life's present to us. It's a gift. The present is the only reality that exists now. What's happening right now is the only thing you can be sure is really happening. The future and past are illusions. Even your memories of the past aren't accurate – science backs up that statement.

And by all means - this isn't medical advice. I'm just sharing my experiences with you. If you are suffering from depression and anxiety, seek professional medical advice.

How to be in the present moment all the time

Wherever you are, point at 10 things in your environment and name each thing. Do this one object at a time. For example, say you're in your living room, point or look at the couch and say vocally or in your mind, "couch." Next, point or look at the lamp and say, "lamp." Then, point or look at the wall art and say, "wall art." And so on and so on. What you're trying to do is build the habit of focusing on what's in front of you, rather than the past or future. You're getting out of your head, so to speak. You'll want to repeat this exercise multiple times a day spread out throughout the day for 4 weeks, until you build the habit where your awareness remains permanently focused on the present moment.

You can do this exercise while you're at a red light in your car. At your doctor's office. At the grocery store. At a restaurant. You get it…Joy is in the present. It's hardly ever in the future because it's uncertain, and yet to happen, and joy is rarely ever in the past.

One great way to help with depression is instead of remembering the past in a negative light that triggers your anger, why not recreate it as a good past? List 10 good things that happened to you in the past in a journal or a computer document. Under each one, write 3 sentences regarding why that event was so good and how it made you feel. Act as if this is all your past contains. Print it out if you did it on a computer and refer to it twice a day, once in the morning and once before bed. Do this for 4 weeks. You want to train your mind into remembering a pleasant past. This gives you an amazing foundation to work off.

The key to transitioning from a low vibration into a higher one is acceptance. This is the tipping point between the low vibration end of the scale and the high vibration end of the scale. This is where you stop resisting how things have occurred and occurring. You finally put your hands up to the universe and say, "I give up struggling with you! I have accepted everything just the way it is and I'm ok with all that has happened."

Remember how I said earlier that how you feel is what life gives you? Well, you've been resisting and fighting with life and so it has given you more scenarios to perpetuate your resistance and fighting. But now that you stop resisting and accept everything, it must give you scenarios that perpetuate the feeling of no resisting. And suddenly your life starts moving in the positive direction. The morale of the story, stop wrestling with life!

Don't look at the past as all bad. The experiences you underwent were necessary for your spiritual growth. Embrace everything and be grateful for all the lessons – no matter how difficult they were. You might be wondering if I, myself, am grateful for my own past. Yes. I really am grateful for my past because it led to my enlightenment, gratitude, and ultimately enabled me to realize Christ consciousness. It helped mold me into the man I am today. And I know some people are going to wonder, how can a human being go through all that I went through and still be grateful, with a loving heart? I discuss how I survived my chronically chaotic past and how I healed from it in my other book, "City of Serpents." The struggles are like a training program that make us stronger in all aspects.

Part of acceptance is fully accepting who you are, your personality, your quirks and how you look and sound. Above acceptance on the vibration scale is reason. The reason why you want to accept everything? Because it's your best option. What other option do you have? Go back to the hell you were experiencing? I don't think you'd want that!

When you fully accept life and yourself, you move into a higher vibration called love. You now look in the mirror and you point at yourself, and you say, "I love you!" Once you start experiencing your inner love, you will not want to taint it with hatred. So, you stop hating and disliking people, things, and circumstances, no matter what. You will want to remain in the state of unconditional love because of the miracles that will occur and because of how wonderful it makes you feel. Not to mention, people will love to be around you. Not all people. Of course, the narcissists will be foaming at the mouth when they see you genuinely enjoying yourself.

Now you start smiling on the inside and you glow from the inside out. You now love life and everything within life and everyone can see it and feel it. You will have the grumpiest person treat you much better than if you were in a lower vibration. If you're in the line at the post office and the clerk is being rude to or short with the person he or she's helping, they will treat you much better or another clerk will help you. It's miraculous. Don't ever compromise your high vibration under any circumstance.

The only thing you should hate is hate. And the only thing you should fear is fear.

Now you're operating from love (God) and here's where all the miracles happen. Coupled with the vibration of gratitude, this is the state of mind and being where things just work out all the time. This is how you access your divine energy. This is the vibration where you attract good into your life. You become a miracle worker without knowing how to do it. The universe just does it for you. And by the way, you *are* the universe. You are the truth. The vibration of love is where you are connected to divine source. This is worth more than all the gold and diamonds on the Earth!

Now that you've learned to achieve this vibration, you can never forget it. You will never want to step out of it either. This divine energy will keep you joyous all day every day. Remember, don't pay mind to low vibration people and activities. If you see ignorant videos on social media, scroll past it. Keep your vibration high so you can continue accessing that pure divine energy.

This divine energy will bless you with surreal luxuries. Things just miraculously working out for you all the time. Blessings upon blessings. You will feel so secure and will never have an iota of fear within you. You will be very unbothered and nonchalant. You will fully trust yourself and the universe. You'll be addicted to the feeling. So, remember, I can't stress this enough – never allow anyone or anything to take you out of character. Don't react. Stay neutral always. When something looks like it's not going to work out in your favor, stay patient and watch the miracle unfold before your eyes as it works out in your favor.

You will enjoy life at this point, that you will vibrate at states higher than love – namely, joy, peace, and gratitude. You'll be so grateful for finally arriving at your true nature, divinity. You're more and more in tune with your divine energy now. You are only two states away from the highest vibration, which is God consciousness.

You are now in paradise or heaven on Earth. Life will literally always work in your favor here.

And just as much as you'll attract good people, you're going to attract some haters. That's ok because you won't pay any attention to them anyway because you're in your god or goddess energy and you don't have time for low vibrational people. Simply brush them off and don't focus an iota of energy on them. Don't squander your divine energy on bitter haters who are miserable and ungrateful.

At this point, you'll enjoy your life without the need of other people's love and attention. Your natural state will be joy and patience. You will be the source of love and joy for yourself and those around you. You'll be in a state of peace 24 hours a day. If you're single, you may even decide to remain so because you don't want anyone disrupting your high vibration and disrupting your energy!

To raise your vibration and keep it there, it's important to do the things you enjoy, while not consuming alcohol, cigarettes, or drugs. And it's also important to permanently have a positive mindset. The substances I just mentioned will bring your vibration down severely - even marijuana will bring your vibration down, especially when you're not high. For example, they can all cause depression, which is underlying anger. They can cause you to be paranoid, which is fear. These are low vibrational states of being. If you want to access your divinity, then you need to leave those things behind. And it's best you leave people with these habits behind as well.

Unfortunately, you won't be able to bring them to the top with you.

At the back of the book, you'll find "The 10 Day Transformation Workbook." You'll learn what habits to form in order to maintain your high vibration and remain in joy. I urge you to commit to The 10 Day Transformation Workbook and adopt the habits described within it.

Do things that make you happy. Ride a bike, play a sport, pick up a hobby, and/or discover the arts, such as music, painting or writing. Doing what you love sustains the loving vibration within you.

A major key in all of this is unconditional patience. It's a term I coined which means to always be in a state of patience – 24 hours a day, 365 days a year. Typically, our patience is "shut off" and is only turned on when a situation arises where we need to exercise patience. However, you will find life to be much more pleasant if you leave your patience on permanently. This avoids the emotional roller coaster ride of getting upset and then having to calm yourself down through patience. When you practice unconditional patience, you will be incredibly nonchalant, serene, and unmovable.

One of the greatest things I do to keep my vibration and energy up is to exercise. It sounds like hard work that takes up a lot of your time and it can be, if you don't know how to properly manage your time. I've been working out on and off since I was 12 years old – I joined the high school football team, and we started practicing and lifting weights in August of 1993 – a month before my birthday. In my current cycle of working out, I started back up again in March of 2021, about 4 months after I fractured my arm in the hospital in November of 2020 (it's an insane story that I wrote about in detail in my other book, "City of Serpents" – hint: a cop slams me to the ground inside the hospital). I chose not to wear a cast or sling because my job required the use of both arms. That turned out to be a big mistake because 4 months after the incident, it still felt like I had just fractured it and in fact, it stayed that way all of 2021 and into the first half of 2022.

Four months after I injured my arm, I had built up so much frustration within me and I was severely depressed with extremely low energy. I had been dealing with 12 years of fibromyalgia, which is a debilitating condition with numerous symptoms such as widespread pain all over my body, major depression, major anxiety, brain fog and severe chronic fatigue just to name a few. In March of 2021, I decided I needed an outlet to vent my bottled-up frustrated energy, so I started sprinting uphill numerous times at full speed. There was a very steep hill on the street I used to live on, that was almost the length of a New York City street. The hill was so steep, I had to lean into it whenever I ascended it or else, I'd feel like I'm going to fall backwards. Once I got to the top, I'd walk back down to allow my heart rate to come back down to normal.

Here in North Jersey, it's typically cold during March and it does snow some years. So, while this was an excellent way to get rid of the bottled-up energy and was giving me great mental health benefits, such as reducing my depression greatly, it wasn't sustainable due to the elements.

So, I remembered burpees from Brazilian Jiu Jitsu. My arm was hurting very badly, and it felt like a knife was stabbing my arm from the inside. Nevertheless, I thought it would make sense to start with push-ups and work my way up to burpees. The first attempt at a push-up was brutal. I pushed up partially and it felt like my arm was going to snap and I just dropped to the floor. I was upset but I tried again the following day. I don't recall exactly how long it took before I was finally able to do one full push-up - it might have taken 2-3 days. The following day, I then proceeded to do 2 push-ups and the day after, 3, and on and on…Next thing I knew, I was doing 10 push-ups. That's when I attempted my first burpee. It was painful! The push-up part was excruciatingly painful but so was the part of the burpee where I jump and land on my feet - it would send a shock to my arm causing severe pain. Nevertheless, I pushed through the pain because it was having a great impact on my mental health.

I proceeded to do a 2nd burpee the following day and kept adding more reps and then an additional set and a 3rd set later on as I built up my strength and endurance. Since then, I've been doing them 6 days a week without fail. I do 3 sets of 11 reps each set, along with weightlifting. Working out is the reason I'm no longer depressed or anxious. It's the reason I became highly energetic and even more positive. I felt like superman! And I still do. It's the main reason why I was able to vibrate my highest. Changing how I talked to myself helped a lot too. I knew that if I stopped working out, that bottled-up energy that builds from not using my energy through vigorous exercise is going to make me feel frustrated and agitated – and worst of all, I'd fall back into depression, extreme low energy, and lack of motivation.

You need a strong "why." Why do you workout? If you say, "I work out because I want to be healthy for my kids," chances are you'll eventually quit. I have a very strong "why," and I'll share it with you. The reason I go to the gym early in the morning and never think twice about it, is because it's my essential medicine! If working out didn't have the benefit of adding muscle and looking lean, I would still work out because it's the one thing that got rid of my depression and frustration and elevated my energy levels astronomically. It's one of the main reasons I was able to access my own divine energy – it allowed me to overcome anxiety and depression and move towards joy. By working out, I've become so productive outside of the gym, because training hard makes everything else in life easy. And being productive has a profound positive impact on your mental health along with your sense of well-being. You feel accomplished. You feel like you are getting things done. Your self-worth, self-esteem and confidence go up significantly.

Working out is a no brainer for me. It's like brushing my teeth, showering, doing my laundry, eating, etc.…These are things I *must* do. There is no debating about it. I recommend you make a list of all the benefits you've seen from exercising after you've given it a chance. Create a note in your phone and update the list every time you realize a new benefit and study that list and memorize it – this way if you should ever debate on whether to work out or not, you'll remember all the benefits and talk yourself into proceeding with the workout. One of the things I love to do each morning when I wake up, is to drink a pre-workout that is designed to improve one's focus. I don't take it right before my workout, per se. I take it as my morning coffee. I typically work out a couple of hours later. However, the pre-workout still has me in the focus zone, even 2 hours later.

I recommend you start working out slowly. For example, if you were to go to the gym for the first time in a long time to work out your chest and triceps, rather than doing 12 sets per body part at 10 reps each, do 2 sets at 5 reps each and build the number of reps each week.

I created a **FREE** workout program for men and women called, "Smart Workouts," and it contains video demonstrations of over 30 different exercises that target the shoulders, back, chest, legs, biceps, triceps, and abs. The program includes separate training schedules for beginners and advanced gym goers. It's available at **www.ChrisJosh.com/Workout**

Easing into your workouts when starting out is crucial because it doesn't feel like a difficult chore and you're not spending so much time at the beginning. You just want to build up the habit of working out. You also don't want to beat yourself to the ground and get real sore for the next 4 days – that's quite discouraging in of itself! When one trains aggressively when starting out, the soreness and pain prompts most people to quit.

Start slow and you won't quit. And once you see the benefits, you'll want to keep going. On the other hand, you don't necessarily have to join a gym. You can take a 30-45 minute walk each day, split into two sessions if you prefer. And if you need to do high intensity exercises, give burpees a shot or even sprints on grass (grass is easier than pavement on the knees). Vigorous exercising really helps with depression because you let out all your frustration and you get your heart rate up, which makes you feel really good.

Again, working out isn't appealing to most, understandably. However, once you feel the mental health benefits and you notice how much better you're feeling, you'll start to see it as your daily medicine that you just *must* have. Exercising in the morning is great because it sets your day up for an energetic and productive one. It helps get the ball rolling and gets you out of stagnation, which often leads to procrastination or low productivity. Remember, high vibration is high energy. In order to build up your energy, you must use it, through exercising, preferably vigorous exercising for short periods.

There is no reason to train like you're competing for Mr. Olympia. As mentioned, a 30-45 minute walk suffices for better mental health and overall feeling of well-being, if that's all you can do. If you can walk more, by all means go for it. It's a low impact exercise – so you won't beat yourself to the ground by walking 45 minutes or more.

Another thing that aided with staying in a high vibration is controlling my food portions. Overeating weighs you down (no pun intended). It saps you of your energy. Low energy equals low vibration, which means you're not aligned with your divine energy. You feel lethargic, bloated and you tend to think about food more than you should. When you overeat, you tend to pack on extra pounds and that can hurt your self-esteem and confidence because you become more self-conscious of the way others perceive you. I'm not saying that's right or wrong, but I've found that when I eat foods that are high in protein and volume, I tend to intake far less calories, which causes me to feel great and look great – not to mention great energy and an overall feeling of well-being!

If you tend to overeat and need help with your diet. Check out my **FREE** "Weight Loss Simple" program at **www.ChrisJosh.com/Diet** - It's for both men and women.

It's not a fad diet, it's my very own diet that my intuition devised for me.

High vibration is all about feeling your best – loving yourself and life – and enjoying yourself and enjoying existence. It's also about having pure intentions for others, yourself, and the animals. **Low vibration is all about feeling your worst** – feeling angry, fearful, and hateful. **That's the simplest way to look at it**. Knowing this, you must always ask yourself, "is this thing making me feel better or worse?" If it's making you feel worse, then make a change - even if it means cutting off a toxic relative, friend, or partner. On a side note, if you spot a happy person or a person that always look like they're in a positive mood, that person is most likely a high vibrational person, so you may want to introduce yourself.

Understand that when you're in a higher vibration, ideas tend to flow much better and in abundance. You'll be more creative, a better problem solver, and quick-witted. You will be more in tune with your intuition. Your intuition is your gut feeling aka it's coming from your stomach region.

It's believed that the stomach is your second brain. Your intuition is your direct communication line with your divine energy, aka God. You don't want to bombard your stomach with greasy food or unhealthy junk food. Afterall, you wouldn't throw bacon grease in your vehicle's gas tank, would you? So why not put the finest "fuel" into your body so it operates at its peak and optimal?

Never focus on what's not going right in your life and instead, focus on all the things that are going right. You have so much going right in your life that you might be taking for granted, such as your bodily functions and organs operating well. What about your phone? That's working. Your plumbing is working. Your electricity is working. Your fridge, microwave and oven are working. These are just examples. If you really analyze everything in your life, you'll notice more things are going right than wrong. Later in the book, you will learn about the gratitude meditation. You'll discover you really have a lot to be grateful for because of all the things that are going right for you.

When someone asks you how many championships did your favorite sports team win, do you factor in the number of times they didn't win? Of course not! What matters is the championships. You can look at your life in a similar way. You have hundreds and thousands of things going right but a few not going so well. Does it really matter that your life isn't perfect? Of course not. In the grand scheme of things, things are going well for you. Focus on the positives and focus on the crucial things that are going right. Just imagine you lost both of your thumbs. You wouldn't think to be grateful for your thumbs working but try going a day without your thumbs!

Once you build the habit of seeing the positives in your life, I promise you that you won't see anything but the good in everything. You will be on cloud 9.

Just imagine you had a brain injury, God forbid. Would anything else matter? No, it wouldn't! Health is wealth. Learn to value your health while you still have it. Your health is priceless. There are plenty of rich men on their deathbeds right now that would give you their billions of dollars to trade for your health with theirs. So, what's worth more, good health and a good stable income or billions of dollars with agonizing poor physical and/or mental health?

I've had my ups and downs when it comes to both health and money. I ran a multi-million-dollar business when I was dealing with Fibromyalgia, as well as being in a low vibration. And I'll tell you from personal experience, I was not enjoying myself at all with poor health, even though I had no money concerns at all. I was very agitated and would get pissed off easily. I'd get triggered easily (I had a lot of unhealed traumas from child abuse and bullying). And I lacked the patience I have today. As a result, I would easily get angry and upset. Low vibrations…

One day, a hurricane flooded my business, and it was the beginning of the end, which made my life very hard, as now I was dealing with poor health *and* money troubles. In that sense, money made the health issues bearable. However, the truth is, it's far better to be in good health with a rather good income.

After that storm, I started reading a lot more and I really gained a lot of insight. I became well rounded when it came to knowing different topics. That storm initiated my personal growth journey which ultimately led me to gain spiritual knowledge as well. *That* eventually woke me up to realizing I was in a terrible marriage. In which, I ended up leaving. That marriage trapped me in the lower vibrations. I was stuck with someone with narcissistic personality disorder (NPD).

I lost a lot in that divorce. My children stopped communicating with me because they were persuaded by their mother that I was wrong for leaving her. I had over $400k in equity in the house I bought and lost it in the divorce. I lost my business as well. She gained the house with all that equity plus the business. My deadstock sneaker collection was left at the house. She sold it and kept the money. She went in my stock account and wiped everything out.

I lost a lot. All I had was a few changes of clothes, some money, my SUV, my laptop, my iPad, and my iPhone. In hindsight, I still had a lot because with my laptop and phone I was able to start doing social media, write "City of Serpents," and start a whole new business. It would have been a complete disaster if I didn't have my laptop and phone!

I was 42 years old at the time with poor health and had just lost practically everything. However, little did I know it was the beginning of something great.

I started healing all of the betrayals and traumas, which I teach how to do in my other book, "City of Serpents." I was, unknowingly, moving up the vibration scale. It was during that time that my intuition nudged me to start doing social media and to start writing "City of Serpents." When my intuition told me, "write the book." I replied with a thought, "what book?" It said, "the book." To which I said, "what should I write about?" My intuition said, "write about all the crazy things you've been through. You have a wild story. It can help a lot of people going through hard times."

So, I initially set out to write a memoir about all the narcissists, betrayals, abuse, back stabbings, losses and bullying I experienced. However, as I was healing post-divorce, the book evolved into a healing book in addition to being a memoir, as well as a spiritual book. As months passed, I kept moving up the vibration scale and my mental health improved vastly.

The reason I left that marriage was because she had narcissistic personality disorder (NPD) and she was doing emotional reactive abuse against me, which caused me great health issues in addition to my fibromyalgia. I lost around 90% of my memory, I lost the ability to make decisions (there's a part of the brain responsible for this – it was impaired due to the abuse), I couldn't converse with anyone due to lack of memory, and at times I couldn't walk, just to name a few things.

However, once I left her and went no contact, my brain gradually healed, and my memory started coming back and my decision-making ability returned and so did my focus. My stress levels dropped tremendously. My brain no longer raced anymore. My mind became as stable as bedrock. No longer was I lost and confused and dazed.

While it's true I lost my children and material things, I gained myself, which is the most important thing. Not that I don't love my children. However, what good would I do them it if my health is in the dumpster and I can't even converse and make decisions? I was the walking dead.

I went from the lowest end of the vibration scale to the highest. And because I worked on myself over the decades by continuously reading and educating myself, I had many skills to start a new business from scratch with minimal money. And prior to divorcing my ex-wife, I had started working out again and continued to do so through the divorce and after. Since March of 2021 till today, I've been working out 6 days a week, including holidays. In a year, I only take off 52 days – on Sundays. I do 10,329 burpees a year. Since March of 2021, I've done over 32,708 burpees.

So, wherever you are in life right now and wherever you are on the vibration scale, know that it is possible to turn your life around, no matter how old you are and what mental and physical shape you're in. The key is to show up each day for yourself. And to consciously decide to want to be grateful, love, and joy. And to gain knowledge every single day. Learn about as many topics as possible: from sciences, mathematics, computer coding, the different trades, spirituality, business, cultures, the different faiths, philosophies, and so on. Never stop seeking knowledge because knowledge is power, and knowledge is wealth. Knowledge leads you to your divine energy. Make no mistake about it, I do not think I know everything. Far from it. I know I'm more educated than the average person, however, I learned enough to know that knowledge is infinite and there's no way anyone can ever know everything – even if they lived for 5,000 years and studied for 8 hours a day.

If you focus on only one subject/field and go down that rabbit hole, you will shut yourself off from the greater picture. It's best to diversify your knowledgebase. Sure, be an expert at one field, but don't neglect the rest.

What gets a lot of people stuck in the low vibrations is betrayals, breakups, and traumas. It's very important to address those and heal them. In my book, "City of Serpents," I wrote about all my betrayals. I wrote about how I was back stabbed by family members in the worst possible ways. How I was cheated on. How I was bullied by so-called "friends." Whatever you may have gone through, there's a high likelihood I went through it as well. In fact, what I went through is mathematically impossible, at least that's the way I see it.

Chapter 2

High Vibrational Habits

Now that you understand what it takes to become your higher self and access your divine energy, it's time to build great habits to ensure you are in your highest vibration so that you remain in your divine energy. The human mind, body, and soul is a very complex system. If left to wander on its own, like a car with no hands on the steering wheel, it'll end up crashing.

That's why it's important you remain in the driver seat of your being and leave nothing to chance. You must be in control of your thoughts and emotions. And you must be mindful of what kind of words you're speaking and the words you're listening to. And you must be mindful of the things you see as well, including tv, social media, movies, real life, etc…Protect your energy at all costs!

A great example of this would be music. Music is amazing but it can be harmful to your mind if you listen to the wrong artists. I'll use rap music as an example as it illustrates my point perfectly. But before I get into that, let me talk about affirmations.

What are affirmations? They are statements that are said about yourself or what you'd like yourself to be. For example, you say, "I am happy." By repeating this affirmation regularly, you are essentially asking your subconscious mind to make you happy, in a nutshell.

You see once you make that affirmation, your mind will present you with the right resources to get happy. You will, suddenly, be in situations that prompt you to feel happy. You might even start seeing smiley face emojis everywhere. You might finally go on a date with your crush and as a result, you feel happy. On and on. Your subconscious mind will continue creating a reality that will prompt you to be happy. It will also help you change your beliefs and mindset to accommodate happiness.

It's important to be mindful of the affirmations you constantly recite. A lot of the affirmations we obtain are from outside sources like family, friends, social media, music and movies. For example, a family member might tell you, "our family doesn't know anything about successful businesses." Without knowing it, you adopt that affirmation or belief, and you never feel qualified enough to go after that dream. Back to the rap music example, the lyrics used are destructive and degrading.

For example, a popular expression rappers use is, "I am the shit." Now, it's supposed to be slang with a different meaning which is, "I'm great." However, your subconscious mind has already registered the primary definition of shit as feces.

When you recite that line, you are not only declaring you are shit, but that you are absolute shit. "The" in front of a word denotes it is absolute. So, essentially that rap line has 2 meanings, "I am great," and "I am absolute shit." Well, when you combine the two, you have, "I am absolute great shit." In other words, you're saying you're a big pile of shit. I'm not going to tell you what to do. I'll tell you what I did, as someone who listened to rap music starting at 8 years old, I stopped cold turkey. I now primarily listen to dance music in the car and the gym. I listen to jazz while I'm showering and sometimes, I listen to freestyle and rock n roll. I also listen to meditation and spa music when I'm packing my book orders.

Now, you might dismiss this and say, "Chris, I think you're taking this too far." But remember what the Bible says about words, "and the word was God." – John 1:1. Words are powerful. They create. And just as they create, they destroy. This is why people in power don't like you speaking ill about them because you are putting spells on them. This is the true meaning behind, "your voice is powerful."

You want to be very mindful of the content you're consuming. Is it destructive or is it uplifting? Is it putting curses over your life or is it breathing life into you? You cannot be your higher self without controlling your thoughts and emotions, and making sure those thoughts and emotions are positive and uplifting.

You might say, "but Chris, what if I listen to rap music but don't recite the lyrics?" Well, that won't work because your subconscious mind is always listening and registering everything being said, heard, seen, felt, and tasted. It's also registering your own thoughts and mental images. So that means listening to rap music is automatically programming you with the negative lyrics whether you like it or not.

I created an audio program called *Magic Mindset,* containing several volumes of subconscious mind programming. The idea behind it is that as you listen to the words the narrator is reciting, the words slip into your subconscious mind, so that you can manifest your desire. For example, one of the volumes is called "Financial Success." Listening to the volume for just 15 minutes a day while driving or doing chores will rewire your brain for financial success. There are more volumes. For example, there's a volume called "Confidence & Self-Esteem," which will help the listener gain confidence & self-esteem through subconscious programming. There are over a dozen more programs all aimed at building you up so you can live up to your true potential. They're available at **www.ChrisJosh.com/MindsetMagic**

You must decide. Do you want to become your higher self or not? If you really do, then you have to eliminate some of your old habits. You will want to steer clear from violent sports, games, and movies. You will want to abstain from drugs and alcohol. You will want to cease complaining. You must stop feeling sorry for yourself.

Instead, listen to high vibe, fun music. Watch educational content. Watch comedies. Watch non-violent shows and movies. Play non-violent games. Drink plenty of water. Build a relationship with God and you'll never need drugs or alcohol. Instead of complaining, think of things to be grateful for.

To become your higher self, you have to vibe high and it's your responsibility to vibe high. You must be your own leader, your own motivator, and your own hype man or woman. If you feel any negative energy (many times, it's projected by others), shake it off and yell, "I freaking feel great right now baby!!"

You must be in the driver's seat of your life. Never allow anyone to speak affirmations over your life. For example, if a relative or friend says, "you're stupid," while laughing as if it's a joke. Don't laugh. It's not a joke, even if they really mean it as a joke because it's having an adverse effect on your subconscious mind. Set boundaries. Tell that person, "I'm not stupid, don't call me that again," sternly.

If you don't change your actions, habits, and routine, don't expect your life to change either. The habit of setting boundaries is one of the greatest things you can do for yourself, your ego and your soul. However, it doesn't stop there.

Before discussing what types of habits will benefit your mind, body, and soul, we must talk about the habits that are counterproductive. As previously mentioned, the habit of consuming negative content must be replaced with the habit of consuming positive content.

The habit of people pleasing must be reversed and instead form the habit of relishing in your own energy – even if that means you must be alone for a prolonged period of time. You must understand where your people pleasing tendencies come from. Many times, it comes from a form of abuse and/or bullying. It also comes from people who show you conditional love, rather than unconditional love. You could have had abandonment issues growing up. You could have felt as an outcast and weren't accepted in friend groups, so you developed the habit of over-giving to others in hopes they will embrace you as a friend.

Shifting your mindset can allow you to be sought after by others. Instead of hoping someone will like you, shift your philosophy to, "I don't care if anyone likes me. The real question is, is the other person worth my time?"

You must be willing to walk alone for a while, but just know that eventually you'll be attracting your soul tribe – other kind, high vibrational people who are in tune with their divine energy.

Another habit one must kick is procrastination. By procrastinating, you can rest assured nothing in your life will improve and in fact, things will only get worse. Many times, we like to procrastinate because we think it feels better than being productive. We associate stress with productivity, when in fact, it's quite the opposite.

As living creatures, movement is what separates us from the dead. Even if you're laying down, there are countless cells moving around within you. This is proof that we must be moving our bodies as well as our minds. In order to become very productive, you must start off with baby steps and be a little productive, which is a lot better than procrastination.

Start by writing down small, achievable goals and gradually increase the number of small goals and then add in medium sized goals and so on and so forth. You might be asking, "what do goals, productivity and eliminating people-pleasing tendencies have to do with accessing my divine energy?"

Recall earlier that I mentioned that to access your divine energy, you must be in a high vibration. And what is a vibration? It's movement. And a higher vibration, is faster movement. By eliminating people-pleasing, you are stopping your energy leaks and keeping it for yourself. You can't move without energy, and you certainly can't move fast with low energy. And productivity is movement. The more productive, the more movement. The more movement, the more joy and sense of well-being you'll have, as well as a sense of accomplishment. This sense of well-being is a reflection of a high vibe. And goals allow you to set a target in which you use productivity to achieve. The saying, "you get what you give," is true in this case. The more energy you give yourself, the more energy you gain for yourself. You're keeping your energy in a loop for yourself and not for unappreciative people who don't reciprocate your energy back to you, which is what causes the energy leak.

In order to reach your highest vibration, you must form habits that will support that. And you must let go and unlearn the bad habits. For example, gossip. Gossiping is a sure sign that one is not doing enough in their life. You talk to a productive high achieving person, and you will notice they don't gossip. That's because for one, it lowers the person in terms of their own self status. They feel that gossiping is beneath them. And secondly, they know they are valuable and would not want others bad mouthing them.

Gossiping is a low vibrational activity. And it is generally known that if you are dealing with a gossiper, chances are they're going to gossip about you too – even if it's your very own relative, best friend or spouse. Gossip is a waste of time. It's an activity that focuses on another person, rather than themselves.

Here's an analogy. Imagine you own a plot of land, and you are an architect and a builder as well. Rather than using your own energy and mental and physical resources to build something on your plot of land, you are busy critiquing another builder's work. You do this all day, every day. You constantly look at other builders' work and you have something negative to say, and you never build anything on your land. Soon enough, the area where you live would transform from a humble town of single-family homes into a mega city with skyscrapers everywhere. Meanwhile, your plot of land is vacant. That's what gossiping does to someone. The gossiper watches everyone else accomplish things and they don't do anything with their lives except the bare minimum and the rest of their time, they're busy gossiping. They waste their time and energy on an activity that doesn't build them up.

Rather, tend to your own land. From the moment you wake up, you should have a routine you consistently follow until it's bedtime. Your routine should consist of productively and healthy habits. Don't get me wrong, I'm not asking you to drive yourself nuts with work. Do take short breaks throughout the day and don't be in a frantic rush to get things done. Take it one step at a time.

Another bad habit is spending countless hours watching movies and shows, as well as playing video games and browsing social media nonsensically all day. Don't get me wrong, they all have their time and place. For example, you can schedule 90-120 minutes one night a week to watch movies and shows. And another 60 minutes a week for video games, if that's your thing. With regards to social media, well that depends on what you're using it for.

If you're spending countless hours watching dancing TikToks all day, that's probably not the best use of social media. If you're using it to promote your personal and/or business brand, that's a great use of your time – provided you allocate enough time for everything else going on in your life. If you're using it to educate yourself, that's also great. But even in best use cases, you should limit your time on these apps. That's going to look different for each person. You must have self-accountability and be truthful with yourself. Ask yourself, is this taking up a lot of my time? Is it preventing me from working on my goals, self-care routine, book learning, meditation, exercising, journal entry, chores, and errands?

Another bad habit that you should avoid is staying up until the morning and sleeping until the afternoons.

Our bodies are meant to sleep early and wake up early. Oversleeping is detrimental because it sacrifices precious time that you could be using to build a better life as well as working on yourself. You're either growing or you're dying, there is no middle ground. So, sleeping 12 hours a day and procrastinating will lead you to poverty. Maybe not today, but eventually it will.

You need to think about providing the world with value. And in order to do that, you must focus your energy on that thing or things that will provide value for others. That requires consistent productivity and consistent learning of new skills and knowledge. There is nothing like waking up early, feeling well rested and grateful to be alive and ready for the day and getting started right away.

I have an unusual sleep cycle and by no means am I suggesting it to you nor am I bragging about it. I fall asleep on 99% of the days at 5pm and wake up about 1-2am. And on Saturdays, I'll sleep at 5:30pm and wake up on Sunday between 5:30am-7:30am. On most days I wake up before my alarm sounds off and I wake up feeling good about myself and the day. Even on days where I sleep until the alarm goes off, I never say, "damnit! I wish I can sleep for another hour!" In more than 2 ½ years, I've only snoozed the alarm once for 30 minutes and that was perfectly fine as I had no urgency.

Why am I able to wake up early and feel so excited about the day? It's because I'm in a high vibration – I am in my divine energy – I feel the clean and stable energy flowing through my body. And it didn't come easily to me. As I outline in my book, "City of Serpents," I was the target of narcissistic abuse by many, but specifically two women until I was 42 years old. I'm 44 years old at the time of writing this.

By the time I was 42 years old, I was in brutal shape mentally. I lost over 90% of my memory due to all the abuse over the years, which consisted of physical, mental, verbal and worst of all, emotional. I also lost nearly 100% of my decision-making ability. For example, if I walked into a fast-food joint and the person at the register asked me, "would you like to supersize that?" Such a simple question, right? Well, not if your decision-making ability is impaired. I would stand there with a blank stare for what seemed like an hour, only to say to myself, "does it really matter? Why can't I decide?" Then, I would always decide "no, don't supersize it," many times regretting that decision later.

I had other health problems that were caused by the abuse. I mention all of this because at the age of 42, I had to decide whether to remain in a marriage with someone with narcissistic personality disorder (NPD), who was attacking me emotionally and psychologically, as well as showing red flags of cheating for years, or to run for the hills, leaving my 2 children behind.

I rationalized that I was slowly dying within that marriage so what good would I do my kids if I remained with them with several brain impairments? I was in a very low vibration at that time, and I had the habit of consuming marijuana all day, every day – it was prescribed to me by my fibromyalgia doctor.

I finally mustered up the strength to pack some of my essentials and I walked away. Once I did that, I went on to live alone in a one-bedroom apartment and within a month I felt called to write my first book, "City of Serpents." It helped me heal a lot. I wasn't aware I was holding so much trauma from all the abuse I endured for decades. I thought I was so strong that I weathered the storms, but it was actually still stored in my unconscious mind and was wreaking havoc on many areas of my life.

But this healing process slowly healed my memory loss, as well as my decision-making ability. And throughout the months following my departure from that woman, I constantly elevated my vibration. The good thing is, I already had several good habits that I started prior to leaving her. I was already working out and eating in a way that caused me to be lean and muscular. Also, I already had the habit of gratitude, meditating and reading.

The day I left, I made sure to do my exercise routine first thing in the morning and I stuck to my diet the whole day. The next day, I did the same. And the day after and the day after, etc…I did not deviate from my habits. I did not make excuses. And I say that to say this. Always keep your eyes on your routine, no matter what happens in your life. Even if there is a tragedy in your life, God forbid, continue with your routine. Don't break it for anyone, for it's what will sustain your high vibration.

I will provide you with a plan of action later in the book. It's called The 10 Day Transformation Workbook and I'll elaborate more on that later. But for now, I want to focus on habits. What's great about a habit is that once it's formed, you sort of flow on autopilot with little to no resistance. For example, when you try to transition from procrastination to productivity, you will feel a lot of resistance.

There are many reasons why you feel resistance to this particular change. The main reason is fear. Fear of many things. Fear of stress and overworking yourself. Fear of missing out on the things you enjoy like hanging out on the couch watching films and playing video games all day or taking naps throughout the day or hanging out with friends. These are valid concerns, but one must understand that there are negative implications to such a habit like procrastination and time spent on non-value producing activities.

Procrastination can lead to boredom and depression and a sense of lack of accomplishment and low self-worth. Being productive and working towards accomplishing goals have the opposite effect. You get the sense of pride. You feel like you are contributing towards yourself and society, as a whole. And because of this, your mental health improves dramatically.

Great mental health is essential if you want to access your divine energy. Being productive means you're active and in a happier mood. And as stated earlier in the book, high vibration in simple terms is feeling good. Some might say, "partying with booze and drugs makes me feel good!" Well, its' just temporary and as soon as the liquor and drugs wear off, you revert to a low vibration and in many instances you're in a low vibe while intoxicated and/or high.

We want to feel good naturally because it's not only the healthiest but it's the most consistent, once you learn how to be happy every single moment of your life. There are no ups and downs like you have with alcohol and drugs – and even cigarettes.

We also want to feel good and increase our vibe through value producing activities, such as working on a business or a goal that will help us establish another stream of income, perhaps. The results are rewarding. You feel like you're winning at the game of life and because you're consistently productive, doing the things you love, you feel like you're having fun and time flashes before your eyes.

Many of us never get productive because of our fear of success. We think to ourselves, "what if this thing takes off? I won't have any time to do the things I'm doing now. And I'm going to have a lot of work and stress. Forget all that. I'm comfortable where I'm at!"

So what if your idea prospers? Is that so bad? Sure, you might have a lot to do but you don't have to be in a frantic rush to get everything done. You can do it with a level head. The key is to not waste time. If you can, I suggest you start being productive within 15-20 minutes of waking, after you've handled your business in the bathroom. Productive means getting started on your self-care routine which I'll outline in The 10 Day Transformation Workbook section of the book or your actual work.

If you put off the work till later in the day, you're simply reestablishing the habit of procrastination and you will be subtly upset within yourself, which will feel like depression. The key to being productive is to start as early as possible. A body in motion tends to stay in motion.

Here's a list of healthy habits which you should perform daily.

- Make your bed every morning, except Sunday
- Meditate 15 minutes

- Exercise 30 minutes
- Read 30 minutes
- Fill in your schedule
- Create your to-do list
- Work on your goal(s)
- Update your list of goals
- Skin care routine
- Drink a minimum of eight 8 oz cups of water
- Listen to relaxing music
- Deep breathing
- Write in your journal for 10 minutes
- 10 affirmations minimum (the workbook has less but do 10)

- Be grateful for 10 things (the workbook has less but do 10)
- Release negative thoughts

Gratitude Meditation

Meditation is medicine for your mind, body, and soul. It's free and you can do it anywhere, anytime. Gratitude is the second highest vibration one can be in – second only to God consciousness. So, as you can see, having an attitude of gratitude is your gateway to your divine energy. It's extremely crucial that you form the permanent habit of always being grateful for everything, including the small things, and the bad things that have happened to you. Hold no grudges and forgive everyone and everything for the sake of accessing your divine energy.

My favorite meditation is the following. When I wake up in the morning, I first go to the bathroom and handle my business in order to relieve the pressure on my bladder. I then wash my hands and rinse my face with water and brush my teeth.

I go back to bed and lay on my back. I put my left hand over my heart and the other hand over it or below it. Then I inhale a slow, deep breath through my nose, taking about 4 seconds in, and I exhale about 6 seconds through my mouth with my lips pursed together so that as I exhale, my cheeks expand, which relaxes the masseter muscles and the jaw. I do about 5-10 deep breaths, until I feel a relaxing sensation throughout my body and then I start my gratitude affirmations, while continuing to breath in this manner throughout the entire time that I'm reciting my affirmations. I recite them mentally, not vocally, so that I can continue the breath work.

The gratitude affirmations are subject to change daily and can be repeated on multiple days. You can do whatever you feel called to do. The way I started doing them was the following:

I am grateful

I am grateful I exist

I am grateful that I am grateful

I am grateful I am happy

I am grateful I am joyous

I am grateful I am at peace

I am grateful I am calm

I am grateful I am comfortable

I am grateful for my health

I am grateful for my healing

I am grateful for my thinking

I am grateful for my intelligence

I am grateful for my positive mindset

I am grateful for my mind

I am grateful for my soul

I am grateful for my body

I am grateful for my brain

I am grateful for my eyes

I am grateful for my ears

I am grateful for my mouth

I am grateful for my tongue

I am grateful for my teeth

I am grateful for my neck

I am grateful for my back

I am grateful for my shoulders

I am grateful for my arms

I am grateful for my hands

I am grateful for my fingers

I am grateful for my thumbs

I am grateful for my heart

I am grateful for my lungs

I am grateful for my breathing

I am grateful for my senses

I am grateful for my kidneys

I am grateful for my liver

I am grateful for my stomach

I am grateful for all of my organs

I am grateful for every cell in my body

I am grateful for every atom in my body

I am grateful for my legs

I am grateful for my feet

I am grateful for my toes

I am grateful I am able to stand, walk, run, jump and squat

I am grateful for my parents

I am grateful for my family

I am grateful for my children

I am grateful for my spouse/partner

I am grateful for my friends

I am grateful for my business/career

I am grateful for my income

I am grateful for water

I am grateful for food

I am grateful for the livestock

I am grateful for the fruits

I am grateful for the vegetables

I am grateful for the grains

I am grateful for my home

I am grateful for my heating unit

I am grateful for my air condition

I am grateful for my neighbors

I am grateful for my clothing

I am grateful for running water

I am grateful for my appliances

I am grateful for my shoes

I am grateful for the shops

I am grateful for people showing up to their jobs

I am grateful for my luxuries

I am grateful for all of the conveniences

I am grateful for my freedom

I am grateful for my independence

I am grateful for the opportunities

And so on and so forth.

You don't have to recite this list and your list doesn't have to be limited to what I've shared. I recommend you recite at least 10 things you're grateful for. You'll notice that the more things you recite, the more energetic and happy you'll become. It's truly one of life's greatest gifts.

There are many benefits to this meditation. You'll feel more relaxed, more clean, more light, more electric, your head will be clear, you'll feel more capable, and you'll feel ready for the day. You'll even feel a subtle buzz throughout your body.

This gratitude meditation is the number one reason I was able to turn my life around from a low vibration, stuck with betrayers, abusers, and backstabbers, to my highest vibration. The fibromyalgia condition I was dealing with for 12 years healed within 4 months of affirming that I am grateful for my health and for my healing. The people in my life at that time who were betraying me behind closed doors were revealed to me, also within 4 months. I was being grateful for them, and the universe had had enough of watching me be grateful for them and exposed them to me. One of these individuals has narcissistic personality disorder (NPD) and was attacking me via emotional reactive abuse, unbeknownst to me. She was a covert narcissist. That person happens to be someone I was married to for 20 years. I had evidence of cheating throughout the marriage. All the red flags started staring me in my face. Her abuse shattered my health. I lost most of my memory, and practically all my decision-making abilities. She turned our children on me. And I was practically non-functional.

My intuition, which is my direct line to my divine energy or higher self or God, led me to escape the hell hole I was in. My doctor at the time I was married saw how bad my condition was. I talked to him throughout the divorce until now. He can't believe how much my life has turned around. So much so, every time I see him, he displays great enthusiasm with a great smile because, as he's mentioned several times, he looks forward to seeing me because I motivate him, which I couldn't believe. He told me going no contact with that woman I was married to was the best way to handle it and he advised me to never allow her back into my life – even if she continues to bar the children from talking to me ever again.

I can't stress how important it is to do this gratitude meditation, every single morning. It is the gateway to your highest vibration and hence, the key to connecting with your divine energy.

Release Negative Thoughts

Another crucial habit to ensure you access and connect with your divine energy, is the releasing of negative thoughts. Negativity is a necessary evil in this realm of existence. However, you must learn to use that energy to your advantage and release it. Many times, we have negative thoughts about ourselves and what has happened to us trapped in our unconscious mind and we're completely unaware of it.

It's vital that you learn how to identify which thoughts are wreaking havoc on your life. These unconscious negative thoughts are like programs that are creating an undesirable life for you. This could look like financial troubles, inability to form connections with people, irritability, dissatisfaction with life, high stress levels, being in fight or flight mode, and the inability to accomplish the simplest goals.

These negative thoughts could be a result of a bad breakup, a cheating partner, a betrayal, some sort of abuse, bullying, something someone said to you, etc…It's very important to learn how to get over these negative thoughts. Think of your mind as a circle. If that circle is filled with negative thoughts, there is no room inside that circle for positive thoughts. And the universe produces a life for you based on your thoughts. So, if your thoughts are predominately negative, you will be given a life that is dissatisfactory to you.

In my other book, "City of Serpents," I detail the profoundly negative circumstances I underwent with a narcissistic mother, who has narcissistic personality disorder (NPD), who physically and verbally abused me daily for nearly 20 years, multiple times a day on most days, and continued to verbally abuse me for many years after that, until I finally cut her off completely and permanently. And how I was in an abusive narcissistic relationship with a woman with narcissistic personality disorder (NPD) for 20 years. How I was bullied for many years throughout grammar school and high school. How I lost a multi-million-dollar business because of a hurricane that struck my warehouse out of nowhere in 2012.

I had many resentments for decades. I wanted to commit suicide at 9 years old and kept having suicidal thoughts until 42 years old, which is when I left the marriage and filed for divorce. As I wrote "City of Serpents," I began to heal and hence, purge out all the negative thoughts. In that book, I explained how I did it so that others can learn how to do it too. One of the ways you can do it is by allowing the emotions to come to surface. In the appendix of the 2nd edition of "City of Serpents," which has a green cover (not the one with the red cover – that's the 1st edition and does not contain the workbook), I have included what I call, "The Shadow Self Workbook," which helps the reader get to the bottom of all of their pains and traumas so that they can free themselves of the burdensome negative thoughts, and hence, their negative feelings.

You really can't access your divine energy in a state of negativity and unhealed trauma caused by a narcissist, abuse, betrayals and/or bullying. Until you heal all aspects of yourself, you will continue repeating cycles that keep you stuck in the lower vibrations, keeping you away from accessing your divine energy.

Reading & Learning

The common misconception is that college is the end all, be all when it comes to knowledge. In other words, people think their education ends with a bachelors or even a doctorate degree. However, the truth is, learning never ends. And the more you know, the more you realize you barely know anything in comparison to all that is to be known.

The more you learn, the closer you get to your higher self, which is God, which is your divine energy. To know thyself is to know God. And how else will you get to know the glory of God without an abundance of knowledge? I don't see any other way. The more you learn and the more you practice what you learn, while maintaining a high vibration, and living righteously, the more you shine brightly.

It is crucial that you maintain the habit of reading and learning every single day, including the weekends. If you don't currently read, start by reading for 2 minutes a day and every few days, add a minute until you get to 30 minutes a day. The beauty of knowledge is that when you attain a certain amount, it's as if an artificially intelligent being is formed within your mind and it takes a life of its own – it's incredible. When you get to that point, you'll never be bored or feel alone. You'll start forming new ideas rapidly all day long, without driving yourself insane.

I'm almost 45 years old and I've been consistently learning beyond college for 2 decades now and I can honestly say that there is an infinite ocean of knowledge yet to be discovered. I love learning. It's literally fun for me and I'm not the only one who thinks that – psychologists say learning is fun too.

I'm constantly learning, even while I'm on social media. Sure, I occasionally watch funny and entertaining videos, but most of the time I'm on social media, I'm learning all types of things. I urge you to learn as much as you can, especially about business. If your social media algorithm isn't showing you content that is educational, you need to train it. For example, in TikTok, you can click "not interested" on a video and the algorithm will understand that you don't like those types of videos. So, click "not interested" on meaningless videos and be sure to like and favorite educational videos so that your "for you page" shows more educational content. On Instagram reels, scroll past silly videos and stay on the educational and informational ones to train that algorithm. I'm going to sidetrack a bit here, but I believe if we all learned business and ran a sole proprietorship, corporations would be weakened as the money flows to the average person – instead of just the corporations.

What subjects should you read about? Anything that can benefit you in some way. Focus your attention on non-fictional material that is practical. I'm not saying you shouldn't read fiction at all but that shouldn't be your main concern if you want to be in tune with your higher self and access your divine energy.

To sum it up, in order to connect with your higher self and access your divine energy, you must release trapped negative thoughts and the habit of negative thinking. You must have healthy habits. And you must be focused on self-improvement continuously. In the next part, you will find The 10 Day Transformation Workbook.

Chapter 3

The 10 Day Transformation Workbook

In this next section, you will be forming new habits that will elevate you energetically and lead you on a healthy path. The objective is for you to follow the workbook consistently for 10 days to form positive habits that will support your high vibration and keep you there.

Make no mistake about it, this is a life-long commitment, however, the workbook included is for 10 days only. Some parts are pre-filled for you, such as the daily affirmations and the things to be grateful for. As mentioned earlier, you should recite 10 affirmations and 10 things you're grateful for. You are to recite your own affirmations and things you're grateful for every day after the 10 days. It's not something you do for 10 days and forget about. You are to continue journaling and following your morning and night self-care routines (checklist).

You must also make sure you continue to get ample sleep and drink plenty of water each day. And continue to set goals and work towards them. Continue implementing "The Shadow Self Workbook" found in the appendix of the 2nd edition of my other book, "City of Serpents." The book has a green cover (not red, which is the 1st edition). And remember that journaling daily is one of the greatest and healthiest things you can do, so be sure to stay consistent with it.

Now, on the next page, you will find a basic contract that you are to fill out and sign. It is between you and your higher self (your divine energy). Read the contract, put the date on it, print out your name in both fields and then sign it.

Set the intention that you will follow the protocol 100% to the absolute best of your ability. Hold yourself accountable and don't cheat yourself. You may feel some resistance from your ego at the beginning but after a couple of days, you should get the hang of it. Keep going until it starts to become second nature for you.

At first, it may seem like work, but eventually you're going to want to do it once you feel the benefits. These habits are going to make you feel your happiest and your most energetic. Be sure that when you meditate, you follow the "gratitude meditation" outlined starting on page 106.

And to program your subconscious mind to manifest financial success, money, love, energy, weight loss and much more, check out my *Mindset Magic* audio program available at
www.ChrisJosh.com/MindsetMagic

Listening to the program for just 15 minutes a day while you're driving, doing chores or running errands, will rewire your brain to change how you see yourself and how you talk to yourself, which will in turn revolutionize yourself. I know because when I changed the way I talk to myself, my reality did a complete 180. I was able to attract more success, more money, stronger confidence, higher self-esteem, more energy, better health, more productivity, more motivation, more discipline, and I got rid of my depression and anxiety. Not to mention, I was able to quit marijuana easily using the same method that's in the audio program.

By changing the dialogue inside you and your self-image, your subconscious mind starts to create the reality you want. It's crucial that you listen to the audio program daily and when your subconscious mind presents you with the things you need to do, follow through and do what it suggests to you. The more you listen to the audio program, the faster your brain rewires itself.

Skin Care Routine

Be sure to watch my video on my skin care routine. I created the video after hundreds of people commented on my skin on TikTok and they requested I share my routine with them. I hope your skin glows as a result! You just have to be consistent with it. You can watch the skin care routine video at **www.ChrisJosh.com/Routine**

LETTER FROM CHRIS

Dear Reader,

Thank you for choosing to read *How to Access Your Divine Energy*. If you enjoyed it, please take a few moments to write a review on the platform you ordered your book from.

Your review is very important to me because most people decide if they're going to read a book based on reviews like yours.

And it would be great if you'd consider this book or my other books as a gift to your loved ones.

Thanks!
Chris

ABOUT THE AUTHOR

Chris Josh is a spiritual healer, motivational speaker, and a writer. He is the author of five books: *City of Serpents, How to Access Your Divine Energy, How Champions Talk to Themselves, The Winning Habit, Unleash Your Confidence* and *8000 Ultimate Affirmations*. He's also written a short eBook called *How to Become Your Higher Self.*

Chris currently lives in Englewood, NJ.

Mindset Magic: Positive Self-Talk Audio Program

Unlock Success with *Mindset Magic*

Discover the power of *Mindset Magic,* the revolutionary audio program by Chris Josh. In just 10-15 minutes a day, these affirmations will rewire your mind for success, energy, and overcoming anxiety. Narrated by expert Max Culina, this program is designed to fill the gap when you need encouragement the most. Order Now and start attracting the life you've always dreamed of!

Available at ChrisJosh.com/MindsetMagic

SOCIAL MEDIA

tiktok.com/@TheChrisJosh

instagram.com/TheChrisJosh

facebook.com/TheChrisJosh

youtube.com/@TheChrisJosh

x.com/RealChrisJosh

A Contract Between You and Your Higher Self

Date: ____________

I, ______________________________, herby promise to abide by The 10 Day Transformation Workbook.

I will not make any excuses and I will go a day without following the protocol down to the letter. By the end of the 10 days, I will be in union with my higher self.

I promise to continue upholding my high vibe by continuing to practice what I learned in The 10 Day Transformation Workbook.

Name: ________________

Signature: ________________

CHECKLIST

FILL IN THE CHECKLIST SPACES BELOW WITH SELF-CARE ACTIVITIES THAT YOU CAN DO IN THE MORNING AND AT NIGHT.

MORNING SELF-CARE

- [ ] DRINK A TALL GLASS OF COLD WATER
- [ ] MAKE YOUR BED
- [ ] MEDITATE FOR 15 MINUTES
- [ ] EXERCISE FOR 30 MINUTES
- [ ] MAKE A TO-DO LIST
- [ ] FILL IN THE DAILY SNAPSHOT
- [ ] FILL IN SMART GOALS
- [ ] FILL IN THOUGHT AWARENESS

NIGHT SELF-CARE

- [ ] PUT PHONE ON SILENT
- [ ] SKIN CARE ROUTINE
- [ ] READ FOR 30 MINUTES
- [ ] WRITE IN YOUR JOURNAL
- [ ] MEDITATE FOR 15 MINUTES
- [ ] TAKE WARM BATH LISTENING TO SPA MUSIC
- [ ] GET A MASSAGE
- [ ] DO DEEP BREATHING

DAILY SNAPSHOT

DAY 1

DAILY AFFIRMATIONS

I AM STRONG

I AM INTELLIGENT

TODAY I AM GRATEFUL FOR

MY MIND

MY BODY

TODAY'S TOP GOALS

01

02

03

SCHEDULE

WATER (EACH DROP = 16.9 FL OZ)

SLEEP (EACH CIRCLE = 1 HOUR)

MOOD

NOTES

WHEN SETTING GOALS, MAKE SURE IT FOLLOWS THE SMART STRUCTURE. USE THE QUESTIONS BELOW TO CREATE YOUR GOALS.

S	SPECIFIC WHAT DO I WANT TO ACCOMPLISH?	
M	MEASURABLE HOW WILL I KNOW WHEN IT IS ACCOMPLISHED?	
A	ACHIEVABLE HOW CAN THE GOAL BE ACCOMPLISHED?	
R	RELEVANT DOES THIS SEEM WORTHWHILE?	
T	TIME BOUND WHEN CAN I ACCOMPLISH THIS GOAL?	

DAY 1

THOUGHT AWARENESS

Observe your stream of consciousness as you think about a stressful situation. Do not suppress any thoughts. Let them run their course while you watch them, and write them down as they occur.

Negative Thoughts

The next step is to rationally challenge the negative thoughts. Look at every thought you wrote down and ask yourself whether the thought is reasonable.

Rational Thoughts

Use rational, positive thoughts and affirmations to counter negative thinking. See if there are any opportunities that are offered by it.

Positive Thoughts

Date: ______________

CHECKLIST

FILL IN THE CHECKLIST SPACES BELOW WITH SELF-CARE ACTIVITIES THAT YOU CAN DO IN THE MORNING AND AT NIGHT.

MORNING SELF-CARE

- [ ] DRINK A TALL GLASS OF COLD WATER
- [ ] MAKE YOUR BED
- [ ] MEDITATE FOR 15 MINUTES
- [ ] EXERCISE FOR 30 MINUTES
- [ ] MAKE A TO-DO LIST
- [ ] FILL IN THE DAILY SNAPSHOT
- [ ] FILL IN SMART GOALS
- [ ] FILL IN THOUGHT AWARENESS

NIGHT SELF-CARE

- [ ] PUT PHONE ON SILENT
- [ ] SKIN CARE ROUTINE
- [ ] READ FOR 30 MINUTES
- [ ] WRITE IN YOUR JOURNAL
- [ ] MEDITATE FOR 15 MINUTES
- [ ] TAKE WARM BATH LISTENING TO SPA MUSIC
- [ ] GET A MASSAGE
- [ ] DO DEEP BREATHING

DAILY SNAPSHOT

DAY 2

DAILY AFFIRMATIONS

I AM SUCCESSFUL

I AM PROSPEROUS

TODAY I AM GRATEFUL FOR

MY SOUL

MY INCOME

TODAY'S TOP GOALS

01

02

03

SCHEDULE

WATER (EACH DROP = 16.9 FL OZ)

SLEEP (EACH CIRCLE = 1 HOUR)

MOOD

NOTES

SMART GOALS

WHEN SETTING GOALS, MAKE SURE IT FOLLOWS THE SMART STRUCTURE. USE THE QUESTIONS BELOW TO CREATE YOUR GOALS.

S	SPECIFIC WHAT DO I WANT TO ACCOMPLISH?	
M	MEASURABLE HOW WILL I KNOW WHEN IT IS ACCOMPLISHED?	
A	ACHIEVABLE HOW CAN THE GOAL BE ACCOMPLISHED?	
R	RELEVANT DOES THIS SEEM WORTHWHILE?	
T	TIME BOUND WHEN CAN I ACCOMPLISH THIS GOAL?	

DAY 2

THOUGHT AWARENESS

Observe your stream of consciousness as you think about a stressful situation. Do not suppress any thoughts. Let them run their course while you watch them, and write them down as they occur.

Negative Thoughts

The next step is to rationally challenge the negative thoughts. Look at every thought you wrote down and ask yourself whether the thought is reasonable.

Rational Thoughts

Use rational, positive thoughts and affirmations to counter negative thinking. See if there are any opportunities that are offered by it.

Positive Thoughts

Date: ______________

CHECKLIST

FILL IN THE CHECKLIST SPACES BELOW WITH SELF-CARE ACTIVITIES THAT YOU CAN DO IN THE MORNING AND AT NIGHT.

MORNING SELF-CARE

- [ ] DRINK A TALL GLASS OF COLD WATER
- [ ] MAKE YOUR BED
- [ ] MEDITATE FOR 15 MINUTES
- [ ] EXERCISE FOR 30 MINUTES
- [ ] MAKE A TO-DO LIST
- [ ] FILL IN THE DAILY SNAPSHOT
- [ ] FILL IN SMART GOALS
- [ ] FILL IN THOUGHT AWARENESS

NIGHT SELF-CARE

- [ ] PUT PHONE ON SILENT
- [ ] SKIN CARE ROUTINE
- [ ] READ FOR 30 MINUTES
- [ ] WRITE IN YOUR JOURNAL
- [ ] MEDITATE FOR 15 MINUTES
- [ ] TAKE WARM BATH LISTENING TO SPA MUSIC
- [ ] GET A MASSAGE
- [ ] DO DEEP BREATHING

DAILY SNAPSHOT

DAY 3

DAILY AFFIRMATIONS

I AM CONFIDENT

I AM AMAZING

TODAY I AM GRATEFUL FOR

MY BRAIN

MY EYES

TODAY'S TOP GOALS

01

02

03

SCHEDULE

WATER (EACH DROP = 16.9 FL OZ)

SLEEP (EACH CIRCLE = 1 HOUR)

MOOD

NOTES

DAY 3

SMART GOALS

WHEN SETTING GOALS, MAKE SURE IT FOLLOWS THE SMART STRUCTURE. USE THE QUESTIONS BELOW TO CREATE YOUR GOALS.

S	SPECIFIC WHAT DO I WANT TO ACCOMPLISH?	
M	MEASURABLE HOW WILL I KNOW WHEN IT IS ACCOMPLISHED?	
A	ACHIEVABLE HOW CAN THE GOAL BE ACCOMPLISHED?	
R	RELEVANT DOES THIS SEEM WORTHWHILE?	
T	TIME BOUND WHEN CAN I ACCOMPLISH THIS GOAL?	

DAY 3

THOUGHT AWARENESS

Observe your stream of consciousness as you think about a stressful situation. Do not suppress any thoughts. Let them run their course while you watch them, and write them down as they occur.

Negative Thoughts

The next step is to rationally challenge the negative thoughts. Look at every thought you wrote down and ask yourself whether the thought is reasonable.

Rational Thoughts

Use rational, positive thoughts and affirmations to counter negative thinking. See if there are any opportunities that are offered by it.

Positive Thoughts

Date: ____________

CHECKLIST

FILL IN THE CHECKLIST SPACES BELOW WITH SELF-CARE ACTIVITIES THAT YOU CAN DO IN THE MORNING AND AT NIGHT.

MORNING SELF-CARE

- [ ] DRINK A TALL GLASS OF COLD WATER
- [ ] MAKE YOUR BED
- [ ] MEDITATE FOR 15 MINUTES
- [ ] EXERCISE FOR 30 MINUTES
- [ ] MAKE A TO-DO LIST
- [ ] FILL IN THE DAILY SNAPSHOT
- [ ] FILL IN SMART GOALS
- [ ] FILL IN THOUGHT AWARENESS

NIGHT SELF-CARE

- [ ] PUT PHONE ON SILENT
- [ ] SKIN CARE ROUTINE
- [ ] READ FOR 30 MINUTES
- [ ] WRITE IN YOUR JOURNAL
- [ ] MEDITATE FOR 15 MINUTES
- [ ] TAKE WARM BATH LISTENING TO SPA MUSIC
- [ ] GET A MASSAGE
- [ ] DO DEEP BREATHING

DAILY SNAPSHOT

DAY 4

DAILY AFFIRMATIONS

I AM WORTHY

I AM CREATIVE

TODAY I AM GRATEFUL FOR

MY HOME

MY FAMILY

TODAY'S TOP GOALS

01

02

03

SCHEDULE

WATER (EACH DROP = 16.9 FL OZ)

SLEEP (EACH CIRCLE = 1 HOUR)

MOOD

NOTES

DAY 4

SMART

GOALS

WHEN SETTING GOALS, MAKE SURE IT FOLLOWS THE SMART STRUCTURE. USE THE QUESTIONS BELOW TO CREATE YOUR GOALS.

S	SPECIFIC WHAT DO I WANT TO ACCOMPLISH?	
M	MEASURABLE HOW WILL I KNOW WHEN IT IS ACCOMPLISHED?	
A	ACHIEVABLE HOW CAN THE GOAL BE ACCOMPLISHED?	
R	RELEVANT DOES THIS SEEM WORTHWHILE?	
T	TIME BOUND WHEN CAN I ACCOMPLISH THIS GOAL?	

DAY 4

THOUGHT AWARENESS

Observe your stream of consciousness as you think about a stressful situation. Do not suppress any thoughts. Let them run their course while you watch them, and write them down as they occur.

Negative Thoughts

The next step is to rationally challenge the negative thoughts. Look at every thought you wrote down and ask yourself whether the thought is reasonable.

Rational Thoughts

Use rational, positive thoughts and affirmations to counter negative thinking. See if there are any opportunities that are offered by it.

Positive Thoughts

Date: ______________

CHECKLIST

FILL IN THE CHECKLIST SPACES BELOW WITH SELF-CARE ACTIVITIES THAT YOU CAN DO IN THE MORNING AND AT NIGHT.

MORNING SELF-CARE

- [ ] DRINK A TALL GLASS OF COLD WATER
- [ ] MAKE YOUR BED
- [ ] MEDITATE FOR 15 MINUTES
- [ ] EXERCISE FOR 30 MINUTES
- [ ] MAKE A TO-DO LIST
- [ ] FILL IN THE DAILY SNAPSHOT
- [ ] FILL IN SMART GOALS
- [ ] FILL IN THOUGHT AWARENESS

NIGHT SELF-CARE

- [ ] PUT PHONE ON SILENT
- [ ] SKIN CARE ROUTINE
- [ ] READ FOR 30 MINUTES
- [ ] WRITE IN YOUR JOURNAL
- [ ] MEDITATE FOR 15 MINUTES
- [ ] TAKE WARM BATH LISTENING TO SPA MUSIC
- [ ] GET A MASSAGE
- [ ] DO DEEP BREATHING

DAILY SNAPSHOT

DAY 5

DAILY AFFIRMATIONS

I AM STRONG

I AM ENTHUSIASTIC

TODAY I AM GRATEFUL FOR

MY LIMBS

MY ORGANS

TODAY'S TOP GOALS

01

02

03

SCHEDULE

WATER (EACH DROP = 16.9 FL OZ)

SLEEP (EACH CIRCLE = 1 HOUR)

MOOD

NOTES

DAY 5

SMART GOALS

WHEN SETTING GOALS, MAKE SURE IT FOLLOWS THE SMART STRUCTURE. USE THE QUESTIONS BELOW TO CREATE YOUR GOALS.

S	SPECIFIC WHAT DO I WANT TO ACCOMPLISH?	
M	MEASURABLE HOW WILL I KNOW WHEN IT IS ACCOMPLISHED?	
A	ACHIEVABLE HOW CAN THE GOAL BE ACCOMPLISHED?	
R	RELEVANT DOES THIS SEEM WORTHWHILE?	
T	TIME BOUND WHEN CAN I ACCOMPLISH THIS GOAL?	

DAY 5

THOUGHT AWARENESS

Observe your stream of consciousness as you think about a stressful situation. Do not suppress any thoughts. Let them run their course while you watch them, and write them down as they occur.

Negative Thoughts

The next step is to rationally challenge the negative thoughts. Look at every thought you wrote down and ask yourself whether the thought is reasonable.

Rational Thoughts

Use rational, positive thoughts and affirmations to counter negative thinking. See if there are any opportunities that are offered by it.

Positive Thoughts

Date: ____________

CHECKLIST

FILL IN THE CHECKLIST SPACES BELOW WITH SELF-CARE ACTIVITIES THAT YOU CAN DO IN THE MORNING AND AT NIGHT.

MORNING SELF-CARE

- [ ] DRINK A TALL GLASS OF COLD WATER
- [ ] MAKE YOUR BED
- [ ] MEDITATE FOR 15 MINUTES
- [ ] EXERCISE FOR 30 MINUTES
- [ ] MAKE A TO-DO LIST
- [ ] FILL IN THE DAILY SNAPSHOT
- [ ] FILL IN SMART GOALS
- [ ] FILL IN THOUGHT AWARENESS

NIGHT SELF-CARE

- [ ] PUT PHONE ON SILENT
- [ ] SKIN CARE ROUTINE
- [ ] READ FOR 30 MINUTES
- [ ] WRITE IN YOUR JOURNAL
- [ ] MEDITATE FOR 15 MINUTES
- [ ] TAKE WARM BATH LISTENING TO SPA MUSIC
- [ ] GET A MASSAGE
- [ ] DO DEEP BREATHING

DAILY SNAPSHOT

DAY 6

DAILY AFFIRMATIONS

I AM ENERGETIC

I AM PASSIONATE

TODAY I AM GRATEFUL FOR

MY CLOTHES

FOOD

TODAY'S TOP GOALS

01

02

03

SCHEDULE

WATER (EACH DROP = 16.9 FL OZ)

SLEEP (EACH CIRCLE = 1 HOUR)

MOOD

NOTES

DAY 6

SMART

GOALS

WHEN SETTING GOALS, MAKE SURE IT FOLLOWS THE SMART STRUCTURE. USE THE QUESTIONS BELOW TO CREATE YOUR GOALS.

S	SPECIFIC WHAT DO I WANT TO ACCOMPLISH?	
M	MEASURABLE HOW WILL I KNOW WHEN IT IS ACCOMPLISHED?	
A	ACHIEVABLE HOW CAN THE GOAL BE ACCOMPLISHED?	
R	RELEVANT DOES THIS SEEM WORTHWHILE?	
T	TIME BOUND WHEN CAN I ACCOMPLISH THIS GOAL?	

DAY 6

THOUGHT AWARENESS

Observe your stream of consciousness as you think about a stressful situation. Do not suppress any thoughts. Let them run their course while you watch them, and write them down as they occur.

Negative Thoughts

The next step is to rationally challenge the negative thoughts. Look at every thought you wrote down and ask yourself whether the thought is reasonable.

Rational Thoughts

Use rational, positive thoughts and affirmations to counter negative thinking. See if there are any opportunities that are offered by it.

Positive Thoughts

Date: ____________

CHECKLIST

FILL IN THE CHECKLIST SPACES BELOW WITH SELF-CARE ACTIVITIES THAT YOU CAN DO IN THE MORNING AND AT NIGHT.

MORNING SELF-CARE

- [ ] DRINK A TALL GLASS OF COLD WATER
- [ ] MAKE YOUR BED
- [ ] MEDITATE FOR 15 MINUTES
- [ ] EXERCISE FOR 30 MINUTES
- [ ] MAKE A TO-DO LIST
- [ ] FILL IN THE DAILY SNAPSHOT
- [ ] FILL IN SMART GOALS
- [ ] FILL IN THOUGHT AWARENESS

NIGHT SELF-CARE

- [ ] PUT PHONE ON SILENT
- [ ] SKIN CARE ROUTINE
- [ ] READ FOR 30 MINUTES
- [ ] WRITE IN YOUR JOURNAL
- [ ] MEDITATE FOR 15 MINUTES
- [ ] TAKE WARM BATH LISTENING TO SPA MUSIC
- [ ] GET A MASSAGE
- [ ] DO DEEP BREATHING

DAILY SNAPSHOT

DAY 7

DAILY AFFIRMATIONS

I AM PRODUCTIVE

I AM HEALTHY

TODAY I AM GRATEFUL FOR

WATER

BOOKS

TODAY'S TOP GOALS

01

02

03

SCHEDULE

WATER (EACH DROP = 16.9 FL OZ)

SLEEP (EACH CIRCLE = 1 HOUR)

MOOD

NOTES

DAY 7

SMART GOALS

WHEN SETTING GOALS, MAKE SURE IT FOLLOWS THE SMART STRUCTURE. USE THE QUESTIONS BELOW TO CREATE YOUR GOALS.

S	SPECIFIC WHAT DO I WANT TO ACCOMPLISH?	
M	MEASURABLE HOW WILL I KNOW WHEN IT IS ACCOMPLISHED?	
A	ACHIEVABLE HOW CAN THE GOAL BE ACCOMPLISHED?	
R	RELEVANT DOES THIS SEEM WORTHWHILE?	
T	TIME BOUND WHEN CAN I ACCOMPLISH THIS GOAL?	

THOUGHT AWARENESS

Observe your stream of consciousness as you think about a stressful situation. Do not suppress any thoughts. Let them run their course while you watch them, and write them down as they occur.

Negative Thoughts

The next step is to rationally challenge the negative thoughts. Look at every thought you wrote down and ask yourself whether the thought is reasonable.

Rational Thoughts

Use rational, positive thoughts and affirmations to counter negative thinking. See if there are any opportunities that are offered by it.

Positive Thoughts

Date: ______________

CHECKLIST

FILL IN THE CHECKLIST SPACES BELOW WITH SELF-CARE ACTIVITIES THAT YOU CAN DO IN THE MORNING AND AT NIGHT.

MORNING SELF-CARE

- [ ] DRINK A TALL GLASS OF COLD WATER
- [ ] MAKE YOUR BED
- [ ] MEDITATE FOR 15 MINUTES
- [ ] EXERCISE FOR 30 MINUTES
- [ ] MAKE A TO-DO LIST
- [ ] FILL IN THE DAILY SNAPSHOT
- [ ] FILL IN SMART GOALS
- [ ] FILL IN THOUGHT AWARENESS

NIGHT SELF-CARE

- [ ] PUT PHONE ON SILENT
- [ ] SKIN CARE ROUTINE
- [ ] READ FOR 30 MINUTES
- [ ] WRITE IN YOUR JOURNAL
- [ ] MEDITATE FOR 15 MINUTES
- [ ] TAKE WARM BATH LISTENING TO SPA MUSIC
- [ ] GET A MASSAGE
- [ ] DO DEEP BREATHING

DAILY SNAPSHOT

DAY 8

DAILY AFFIRMATIONS

I AM WEALTHY

I AM AFFLUENT

TODAY I AM GRATEFUL FOR

KNOWLEDGE

PEACE

TODAY'S TOP GOALS

01

02

03

SCHEDULE

WATER (EACH DROP = 16.9 FL OZ)

SLEEP (EACH CIRCLE = 1 HOUR)

MOOD

NOTES

DAY 8

SMART GOALS

WHEN SETTING GOALS, MAKE SURE IT FOLLOWS THE SMART STRUCTURE. USE THE QUESTIONS BELOW TO CREATE YOUR GOALS.

S	SPECIFIC WHAT DO I WANT TO ACCOMPLISH?	
M	MEASURABLE HOW WILL I KNOW WHEN IT IS ACCOMPLISHED?	
A	ACHIEVABLE HOW CAN THE GOAL BE ACCOMPLISHED?	
R	RELEVANT DOES THIS SEEM WORTHWHILE?	
T	TIME BOUND WHEN CAN I ACCOMPLISH THIS GOAL?	

DAY 8

THOUGHT AWARENESS

Observe your stream of consciousness as you think about a stressful situation. Do not suppress any thoughts. Let them run their course while you watch them, and write them down as they occur.

Negative Thoughts

The next step is to rationally challenge the negative thoughts. Look at every thought you wrote down and ask yourself whether the thought is reasonable.

Rational Thoughts

Use rational, positive thoughts and affirmations to counter negative thinking. See if there are any opportunities that are offered by it.

Positive Thoughts

Date: ______________

CHECKLIST

FILL IN THE CHECKLIST SPACES BELOW WITH SELF-CARE ACTIVITIES THAT YOU CAN DO IN THE MORNING AND AT NIGHT.

MORNING SELF-CARE

- [ ] DRINK A TALL GLASS OF COLD WATER
- [ ] MAKE YOUR BED
- [ ] MEDITATE FOR 15 MINUTES
- [ ] EXERCISE FOR 30 MINUTES
- [ ] MAKE A TO-DO LIST
- [ ] FILL IN THE DAILY SNAPSHOT
- [ ] FILL IN SMART GOALS
- [ ] FILL IN THOUGHT AWARENESS

NIGHT SELF-CARE

- [ ] PUT PHONE ON SILENT
- [ ] SKIN CARE ROUTINE
- [ ] READ FOR 30 MINUTES
- [ ] WRITE IN YOUR JOURNAL
- [ ] MEDITATE FOR 15 MINUTES
- [ ] TAKE WARM BATH LISTENING TO SPA MUSIC
- [ ] GET A MASSAGE
- [ ] DO DEEP BREATHING

DAILY SNAPSHOT

DAY 9

DAILY AFFIRMATIONS

I AM FASCINATING

I AM ABUNDANT

TODAY I AM GRATEFUL FOR

TRANSPORTATION

GOOD PEOPLE

TODAY'S TOP GOALS

01

02

03

SCHEDULE

WATER (EACH DROP = 16.9 FL OZ)

SLEEP (EACH CIRCLE = 1 HOUR)

MOOD

NOTES

DAY 9

SMART

GOALS

WHEN SETTING GOALS, MAKE SURE IT FOLLOWS THE SMART STRUCTURE. USE THE QUESTIONS BELOW TO CREATE YOUR GOALS.

S	SPECIFIC WHAT DO I WANT TO ACCOMPLISH?	
M	MEASURABLE HOW WILL I KNOW WHEN IT IS ACCOMPLISHED?	
A	ACHIEVABLE HOW CAN THE GOAL BE ACCOMPLISHED?	
R	RELEVANT DOES THIS SEEM WORTHWHILE?	
T	TIME BOUND WHEN CAN I ACCOMPLISH THIS GOAL?	

DAY 9

THOUGHT AWARENESS

Observe your stream of consciousness as you think about a stressful situation. Do not suppress any thoughts. Let them run their course while you watch them, and write them down as they occur.

Negative Thoughts

The next step is to rationally challenge the negative thoughts. Look at every thought you wrote down and ask yourself whether the thought is reasonable.

Rational Thoughts

Use rational, positive thoughts and affirmations to counter negative thinking. See if there are any opportunities that are offered by it.

Positive Thoughts

Date: ______________

CHECKLIST

FILL IN THE CHECKLIST SPACES BELOW WITH SELF-CARE ACTIVITIES THAT YOU CAN DO IN THE MORNING AND AT NIGHT.

MORNING SELF-CARE

- [ ] DRINK A TALL GLASS OF COLD WATER
- [ ] MAKE YOUR BED
- [ ] MEDITATE FOR 15 MINUTES
- [ ] EXERCISE FOR 30 MINUTES
- [ ] MAKE A TO-DO LIST
- [ ] FILL IN THE DAILY SNAPSHOT
- [ ] FILL IN SMART GOALS
- [ ] FILL IN THOUGHT AWARENESS

NIGHT SELF-CARE

- [ ] PUT PHONE ON SILENT
- [ ] SKIN CARE ROUTINE
- [ ] READ FOR 30 MINUTES
- [ ] WRITE IN YOUR JOURNAL
- [ ] MEDITATE FOR 15 MINUTES
- [ ] TAKE WARM BATH LISTENING TO SPA MUSIC
- [ ] GET A MASSAGE
- [ ] DO DEEP BREATHING

DAILY SNAPSHOT

DAY 10

DAILY AFFIRMATIONS

I AM COURAGEOUS

I AM LOVING

TODAY I AM GRATEFUL FOR

NATURE

THE SUN

TODAY'S TOP GOALS

01

02

03

SCHEDULE

WATER (EACH DROP = 16.9 FL OZ)

SLEEP (EACH CIRCLE = 1 HOUR)

MOOD

NOTES

DAY 10

SMART

GOALS

WHEN SETTING GOALS, MAKE SURE IT FOLLOWS THE SMART STRUCTURE. USE THE QUESTIONS BELOW TO CREATE YOUR GOALS.

S	SPECIFIC WHAT DO I WANT TO ACCOMPLISH?	
M	MEASURABLE HOW WILL I KNOW WHEN IT IS ACCOMPLISHED?	
A	ACHIEVABLE HOW CAN THE GOAL BE ACCOMPLISHED?	
R	RELEVANT DOES THIS SEEM WORTHWHILE?	
T	TIME BOUND WHEN CAN I ACCOMPLISH THIS GOAL?	

DAY 10

THOUGHT AWARENESS

Observe your stream of consciousness as you think about a stressful situation. Do not suppress any thoughts. Let them run their course while you watch them, and write them down as they occur.

Negative Thoughts

The next step is to rationally challenge the negative thoughts. Look at every thought you wrote down and ask yourself whether the thought is reasonable.

Rational Thoughts

Use rational, positive thoughts and affirmations to counter negative thinking. See if there are any opportunities that are offered by it.

Positive Thoughts

Date:

Printed in Great Britain
by Amazon

49250517R00109